Dear Friends,

We are delighted to bring you this collection of recipes from our retreat center at long last! Over the years, our guests have been graced with amazing vegetarian meals created with love and talent by our vegetarian chefs. Finally we are ready to share some of our good heart recipes with you.

At Land of Medicine Buddha, we are propelled by our mission of serving at a retreat center which is "A Center for Healing and Developing a Good Heart." Living with a good and kind heart has naturally extended in our area where there are abundant food options, to serving our guests vegetarian meals. While the health benefits of a vegetarian diet are well documented, it is the good and kind heart, a truly healthy heart, upon which we place our focus.

In addition to being a vegetarian center, we are a green certified business. We are proud to be part of a growing community of eco responsible businesses. As such we continue to refine our menus to allow us to provide more local, seasonal and organic foods. By following this path, we have found another avenue to extend our spiritual value of non-harming into our daily lives.

Finally, when our chefs and kitchen staff are hired, we share with them what we feel is the most important ingredient in all of our meals...love. It is our hope that this love is embraced by you our reader, and shared far and wide.

With heartfelt thanks for all who have visited our center, and contributed in so many ways to our success, we humbly give you our very first "Good Heart Cookbook".

The LMB Cookbook Team:
Rachael Bird – Editor
Philip Collins - Contributing Cook
Cynthia Crossley - Contributing Cook
Rachel Enright - Contributing Cook
Brian Espinoza - Contributing Cook
Jason "Dorje" Greenberg - Graphic Designer, Contributing Cook & Editing
Denice Macy - Center Director
Ronald Malanga -Contributing Cook
Laurie McLaughlin – Editing
Melissa Riggall - Editing
Marti Waite - Contributing Cook & Editing
Venerable Annette - Contributing Cook
Venerable Drimay - Contributing Author / Advisor
Vimal - Contributing Cook

Table of Contents

Table of Contents

Borscht

Serves 6

Ingredients:
1 pound beets peeled and cut into cubes
2 medium onions, diced
2 large carrots, diced
2 stick celery, diced
3/4 pound white cabbage, cut thinly into shreds
2 large potatoes, peeled and cubed
2 Tbsp. olive oil
6 cups vegetable stock, or water
Juice of 1/2 a lemon
3 Tbsp. red wine vinegar
1 Tbsp. each oregano and dill
Salt to taste
Coarsely ground black pepper
Sour cream (optional - NOT VEGAN)

Preparation:
Sauté onion, carrots, cabbage, celery over medium heat in the olive oil, with a pinch of salt in a large soup pot. Add beets, potatoes, and veggie stock or water. Season with oregano, dill, salt and pepper, and bring to a boil. Simmer 15-25 minutes, until the vegetables are tender.

Serve with freshly grated black pepper, a dollop of sour cream, and chopped dill or parsley, if desired.

Recipe by: Rachel Enright

Celery Root Bisque

Serves 6

Ingredients:

3 celery ribs, chopped
2 large onions, chopped
1/2 stick unsalted butter
2 large potatoes, cut into 1 inch cubes
2 lb celery root - peeled with a knife and cut into 1 inch cubes
8 cups water
2 teaspoons salt, or to taste
1/4 teaspoon black pepper, or to taste
1/4 cup heavy cream
1 tsp fresh lemon juice, or to taste
2 cups sliced mushrooms

Preparation:

Cook chopped celery and onions in 1/2 stick butter in a large pot over moderate heat, stirring occasionally, until softened but not browned - about 20 minutes. Add water, potatoes, celery root, salt, and pepper and bring to a boil. Simmer until vegetables are very tender, about 30 minutes.

Purée soup in batches in a blender until smooth, then return to pot.

Stir in cream and reheat bisque over low heat. Add lemon juice. In a heavy skillet over moderately high heat, sauté mushrooms with salt and pepper to taste, stirring until golden brown. Transfer mushrooms with a slotted spoon into the soup. Add salt & pepper, if needed.

Recipe by: Rachel Enright

Coconut vegetable soup

Serves 4-6

Ingredients & Preparation:

Saute until very soft:
1/4 medium red onion
1 1/2 Tbsp grated ginger
1/2 Tbsp minced garlic
1/2 red bell pepper, chopped
1 1/2 tsp oil

Add: 1 can coconut milk and simmer for 15-40 minutes. (The longer you simmer, the more the flavors blend). Puree and set aside.

In a separate large pot sauté:
1/2 chopped onion
1 cloves minced garlic
1 diced carrot
2 diced potatoes
1 diced yams
1 stalk diced celery
1 sliced artichoke (optional)
1 1/2 cups sliced mushrooms
1 cups of chopped cabbage
1 cup frozen corn
1 sliced leek

Cook for about 10 minutes, until onions are translucent and mushrooms are soft. Add 3/4 cup of water and 2 cans of coconut milk to cover the contents.

Now add the blended vegetable mixture to the pot. Bring to a boil, and simmer until potatoes are soft. Add one handful of cilantro and basil leaves (chopped), salt and pepper to taste, and a bit of lime or lemon juice, if desired.

Recipe by: Rachel Enright

Corn Chowder

Serves 6-8

Ingredients:

3 1/2 cups diced Yukon Gold potatoes (peeled if desired)
7 cups vegetable broth
6 cups sweet corn
1 large onion, chopped
2 tsp. corn oil or vegetable oil
2 bay leaves
1 tsp rosemary
1 tsp thyme
1/2 tsp salt
1 tsp pepper

Preparation:

In a large soup pot heat oil. Add onions, rosemary, and thyme and saute until onions are translucent. Add potatoes, vegetable broth, corn, and bay leaves. Bring to a boil and reduce heat.

Simmer for 20 minutes. Remove bay leaves. Blend half to all of the soup in a blender or mash with a potato masher until soup is thick. Stir in salt and pepper to taste, and serve immediately.

Recipe by: Marti Waite

Greek Lemon-Egg Soup

Serves 5-6

Ingredients:
6 cups vegetable stock
1 cup rice
1 whole egg + 2 egg yolks
1/4 cup lemon juice
2 Tbsp chopped parsley
1/2 tsp nutritional yeast

Preparation:
Bring stock to boil. Add rice and cover. Cook until tender, being careful not to overcook. Meanwhile in a large bowl beat eggs & yolks until light and fluffy. Beat in lemon juice. Slowly beat in 1 cup of the stock. Combine egg lemon mix with the rice and stock. Bring to near boil then stir in nutritional yeast and parsley. Salt to taste and serve.

Recipe by: Marti Waite

Gumbo

Serves 6-8

Ingredients:
1 cup white flour
3/4 cup vegetable oil
1 medium onion, diced
1 large bell pepper, diced
4 stalks celery, diced
3 tomatoes, diced
6 cups hot water
1 Tbsp paprika
1 Tbsp salt
1/4 tsp cayenne
4 bay leaves
1 1/2 Tbsp thyme
2 bay leaves
2 cups mushrooms, sliced,
1 package of extra firm tofu, drained and cubed

Preparation:
Preheat oven to 400. Drizzle vegetable oil over the cubed tofu and sprinkle with oregano, chili powder, garlic powder, and cumin. Toss gently and bake for 40-45 minutes, flipping the tofu once, until it is crispy and brown.

Meanwhile, heat 3/4 cups vegetable oil and add the flour. Stir constantly until it is a very dark brown, almost burning (a very dark roux is the secret to good gumbo).
When the roux is dark enough immediately add the onion, bell pepper, celery, and tomatoes, and saute for 10 minutes, stirring constantly. Add mushrooms, cook for about 5 minutes. Then add water and spices. Bring to a boil, lower to medium heat, and cook for 45 minutes.

Recipe by: Rachel Enright

9

Tuscan Bean Soup

Serves 6

Ingredients:
1 cup cannellini beans, soaked overnight
1 Tbsp olive oil
1/2 cup diced yellow onions
3 cloves garlic, minced
1 cup diced canned tomatoes
2 cups water
3 sprigs fresh thyme
1 bay leaf
pinch red chili flakes
salt & pepper, to taste

Preparation:
Place the beans in a medium pot, add water to cover by 2 inches and bring to a boil. Turn the heat down, let simmer for 45 minutes to 1 hour or until tender.

In a large soup pot, heat the olive oil over medium heat. Add the onion and garlic. Season with salt and freshly ground black pepper to taste. Add the diced tomatoes, the cooked and drained beans, and water. Season with thyme, bay leaf, red chili flakes, salt and pepper. Cook for 20 minutes.

Serve the soup in large bowls with grated Parmesan and a slice of toast.

Recipe by: Rachel Enright

Classic Caesar

Serves 4

Ingredients:
3 cloves garlic, peeled
3/4 cup mayonnaise
4 Tbsp capers
3 oz. caper juice
1/4 cup + 2 Tbsp grated Parmesan cheese, divided
1 tsp vegetarian Worcestershire sauce
1 tsp Dijon mustard
1 Tbsp lemon juice
salt to taste - ground black pepper to taste
1 1/2 cup olive oil
2 cups day-old bread, cubed
1 head romaine lettuce, torn into bite-size pieces

Preparation:
Combine garlic in a food processor with mayonnaise, capers, caper juice, 4 tablespoons of the Parmesan cheese, Worcestershire sauce, mustard, and lemon juice and blend while slowly adding 1 cup of olive oil. Season to taste with salt and black pepper. Refrigerate until ready to use.

Heat oven to 350°. Toss the cubed bread with remaining olive oil and coat evenly. Continue tossing and add salt and a generous portion of fresh cracked black peppercorn. Pour onto a sheet pan and spread evenly and place in oven for approximately 8-9 minutes or until golden brown. Remove from oven and set aside.

Place lettuce in a large bowl. Toss with dressing, remaining Parmesan cheese, and seasoned bread cubes. Serve immediately.

Recipe by: Rachel Enright

Green Goddess Dressing:

Serves 6

Ingredients:

1 cup packed parsley
1 cup packed spinach
1/2 a zucchini
1 clove garlic
1/4 cup apple cider vinegar
1/2 cup olive oil
1/2 a lemon
Salt & pepper

Preparation:

In a blender combine parsley, spinach, zucchini, garlic, vinegar and blend till smooth and even. Add oil and taste to see if you need more tartness. If so, add lemon juice. Salt and pepper to taste and serve.

Recipe by: Brian Espanoza

Lemon Caper Vinaigrette
Makes approximately 3/4 cup

Ingredients:
Juice of one lemon
1 Tbsp capers, chopped
1 large garlic clove, crushed
1/2 tsp salt
1 Tbsp honey (or to taste)
1 Tbsp parsley, minced
1/3 cup olive oil
Freshly ground black pepper
2 Tbsp mayonnaise
2 Tbsp sour cream

Preparation:
In a small bowl, whisk lemon juice, chopped capers, crushed garlic, salt, honey and minced parsley. Slowly whisk in olive oil. Add mayonnaise and sour cream. Taste and adjust seasonings.

Recipe by: Rachel Enright

Quinoa Salad

Serves 4

Ingredients:
1 1/2 cups water
3/4 cup uncooked quinoa
2 carrots peeled in small cubes
3/4 large green bell pepper, diced
3/4 large red bell pepper, diced
2 stalks of celery, diced
1/4 cup plus 2 Tbsp chopped kalamata olives
3 Tbsp chopped fresh parsley
3 Tbsp chopped fresh chives
1/4 tsp salt
1/2 cup fresh lemon juice
2 1/4 tsp red wine vinegar
3 Tbsp olive oil

Preparation:
Bring the water and salt to a boil in a saucepan. Stir in the quinoa, reduce heat to medium-low, cover, and simmer until the quinoa is tender and the water has been absorbed, 15 to 20 minutes. Scrape the quinoa into a large bowl.

Gently stir the carrots, bell pepper, olives, celery, parsley, chives, and salt into the quinoa. Drizzle with the lemon juice, red wine vinegar, and olive oil. Stir until evenly mixed. Serve warm or refrigerate and serve cold.

Recipe by: Brian Espanoza

Wild Arugula Salad with Seared Pears, Feta Cheese, & Honey Orange Vinaigrette

serves 6

Ingredients:
1/4 orange with peel
2 Tbsp honey
1/4 cup unfiltered apple cider vinegar
1 tsp vanilla extract
3/4 cup canola oil
Salt and pepper
10 oz. wild baby arugula
2 pears peeled, cored and sliced into 8 wedges each
6 oz. crumbled feta cheese

Preparation:
Combine orange, honey, apple cider vinegar, and vanilla in a blender. While blending at medium speed slowly add the oil and salt and pepper. Set aside.

Heat a skillet over medium heat and add the canola oil. When the oil is heated, spread the pears in the pan. Cook slowly over medium heat without moving the pears to allow them to caramelize. Check the bottom of the pears for color and, when browned, flip them over and allow for the same caramelizing on the other side. Once this is done drizzle dressing over the arugula, sprinkle feta over the salad, place a few pear wedges on the side and enjoy.

Recipe by: Brian Espanoza

Main Dishes

Apple Radicchio Risotto with Gorgonzola

Serves 6

Ingredients:

2-1/2 cups and 2 tablespoons uncooked Arborio rice
3/4 cup unsalted butter, divided
9 cups vegetable stock
1-1/2 onion, thinly diced
1 cup and 2 Tbsp dry white wine
1 Gala Apple peeled 1 inch chunks
1 cup Raddicchio 1 inch cut chunks
4 Tbsp balsamic vinegar
2-3 oz. Gorgonzola cheese
1/2 cup parsley, finely diced
salt to taste

Preparation:

Melt half of the butter in a medium saucepan over low heat. Simmer the onion in the butter for about 10 minutes. In a separate pan heat 1 Tbsp of oil over medium heat and add 1 cup Gala apple. Allow to sear for 1-2 minutes then stir and add Radicchio. Allow 2 more minutes then deglaze pan with 4 tablespoons of balsamic vinegar and put aside. Saute the rice in the pan with the onion over medium heat for 5 to 7 minutes, or until lightly toasted. Stir constantly so the rice will not stick and burn. Stir in one ladle of vegetable stock, and keep stirring until it is mostly absorbed, ladling and stirring in more of the broth until the rice is almost al dente. Stir remaining butter, 1/2 cup of diced parsley, Gala apple mixture and salt and pepper to taste. Then add Gorgonzola cheese by spooning it into evenly spaced points through out the risotto. Turn off the heat, cover and let sit for 4 or 5 minutes then serve.

Recipe by: Brian Espanoza

Baked Macaroni & Cheese

serves 6-8

Ingredients:
1/2 lb. elbow macaroni
3/4 Cup butter
3 Tbsp flour
1 tsp powdered mustard
4 cups milk
1/2 medium onion, finely diced
1/2 tsp paprika
3 Tbsp flax meal
12 oz. sharp cheddar cheese, shredded
1/2 tsp salt
Fresh black pepper
Topping:
2 Tbsp butter
1/2 cup bread crumbs

Preparation:
Preheat oven to 350°.
In large pot boiling, salted water cook the pasta to al dente.
While the pasta is cooking, melt ¾ cup butter in a large pot. Whisk in the flour and mustard. Cook for about 5 minutes, stirring constantly, until all the lumps are gone. Stir in the milk, onion, and paprika. Simmer for 10 minutes. Whisk in the flax meal until the lumps are gone. Stir in ¾ of the cheese. Season with salt & pepper. Fold the cooked macaroni into the mix and pour into a greased 13x9 pan. Top with the remaining cheese. For topping, melt the butter in a sauté pan and toss the bread crumbs to coat. Top the macaroni with the bread crumbs. Bake for 30 minutes. Remove from oven and rest for five minutes before serving.

Recipe by: Vimal

17

Black beans thyme

Serves 2

Ingredients:

1-2 tbsp extra virgin olive oil
1-4 cloves Garlic
1-4 pinches of thyme (fresh will require less than dried)
1 medium sized tomato
1 3/4 Cup prepared black beans or 1(15 oz) can of black beans
sea salt
1 scallion (green onion)
Optional: dollop of sour cream or yogurt and a pinch of dried parsley.

Preparation:

Start by putting 1 - 2 tbsp of extra virgin olive oil in a small to medium pot on low-medium heat. (if the olive oil starts to smoke then it is getting burnt).

Chop up a few cloves of garlic and add to the oil. Do not let the garlic get too brown - golden is good. Throw in a couple pinches of thyme. Dice up a medium sized fresh tomato and add to the golden garlic. Let the garlic, oil, thyme and tomato simmer briefly.

Use 1&3/4 cups soaked/cooked black beans or open up a 15oz can of organic black beans and drain out most of the water. Add the beans to the pot. Add a few pinches of sea salt. Stir and cover. Let simmer for 5 minutes covered.

Finely chop a scallion and stir it in with the heat off. Salt to taste

Optional: A dollop of Sour Cream or Yogurt is nice on top after plating. A pinch of dried parsley looks nice on top of that.

Recipe by: Jason "Dorje" Greenberg

Delicious Delhi Dahl

Serves 4

Ingredients:
2 cups boiling water
2 tbsp canola, safflower or sunflower oil (any high heat oil)
1 onion
3-5 cloves garlic
1 pinky-finger-tip sized piece of ginger
2 tsp curry powder (not the plant, but the Indian spice mix)
sea salt
7oz diced fire roasted tomatoes (may substitute single large fresh tomato)
1 cup red lentils (the fast kind)
Fresh Cilantro
Fresh Scallion
Optional: powdered cayenne pepper. Yogurt (NOT VEGAN)

Preparation:
Start this adventure by boiling 2 cups of water – you will need it in a few moments. In a (separate) medium Pot add 2 tbsp canola, safflower or sunflower oil (any high heat oil) at just above medium heat. Dice an onion and put in the pot. It will sizzle like crazy. Stir it until it gets golden and turn down to below medium at that point.

Add a few cloves of chopped up garlic and a finely chopped pinky-tip sized piece of ginger. Then stir in a tsp of curry powder. Immediately add a splash of water and stir it in making the ingredients saucy. Then add a few pinches of sea salt. Add in 7oz diced fire roasted tomatoes and stir then cover. (continued...)

Measure out 1 cup of red lentils and stir into pot.

Your water should have boiled by now so measure out 2 cups of boiling water, add to the lentil pot, stir and cover. Keep covered, stirring occasionally for 15 minutes or until the lentils are not hard anymore. If you do not stir regularly it will burn on the bottom. If it looks like all the water has been absorbed and the lentils are not cooked all the way add a little more boiling water and stir.

Chop up, very finely, several stalks of fresh (and washed) cilantro, including some of the stems (not the part at the very bottom though). Also finely chop a scallion including the green and white parts (excluding the roots). Once the lentils are finished, take the pot off the stove and stir in the cilantro and scallions.

Optional: For spice lovers add powdered cayenne to taste. Also once the dhal is placed in the serving bowls you can add a dollop of yogurt to create a nice contrast to the heat.

Recipe by: Jason "Dorje" Greenberg

Eggplant Parmesan

Serves 8-10

Ingredients:
2 eggplants, sliced 3/4 inch thick
2 eggs, beaten with 2 Tbsp water
3 cups bread crumbs
2 cups white flour
Vegetable oil, for frying
5 cups marinara sauce
1 16 oz package Mozzarella cheese, shredded
1/2 cup Parmesan cheese, grated
1/2 tsp dried basil
Salt & Pepper

Preparation:
Preheat oven to 350 degrees.
Dip eggplant slices in white flour, egg, then in bread crumbs. Over medium fire place pan with 1/4 cup oil and bring to full heat. When oil is ready place battered eggplant into pan. Fry both sides until golden brown.

In a 9x13" pan lay one layer of eggplants and spread 1/2 the marinara sauce over the top. Sprinkle mozzarella and Parmesan cheeses. After the first layer is finished repeat process for a second layer and so on until you have used all of the remaining ingredients. Scatter basil on top.

Bake in preheated oven for 35 minutes, or until cheese is golden brown.

Recipe by: Rachel Enright

21

El Chapine (el cha-peen)

Serves 10

Black Beans

Ingredients:
1 lbs. Black Beans
1 Jumbo Yellow Onion
3 cloves Garlic
2 bay leaves

Preparation:
Soak beans over night and rinse out afterward. Place beans in large pot so that only a 1/4 of the pot are taken up. Fill with water to capacity. Add 1 onion peeled and whole, 3 cloves of garlic, and 2 bay leaves. Bring to boil and reduce fire down to a medium flame to maintain a high simmer. Allow beans to cook stirring occasionally until beans are soft. Season them and remove the bay leaves. Ready to serve.

Plantains

Ingredients:
4 Ripe Plantains (Skin has turned almost completely black and meat has softened)
4 Tblspn Oil
1 cup Creme Fraiche

Preparation:
Add oil to skillet or large pan and heat over medium heat till oil is hot enough to fry on. Peel plantains and slice into 1/4 inch medallions at an angle so they appear long rather than circular. Place them in the oil and allow to crisp up till they have a golden surface to them then turn them over and allow them to fry on the other side. Once they're fried remove from fire and sprinkle a small amount of sugar over them and serve with a dollop of creme fraiche...

...(El Chapine Continued)

Handmade Corn Tortillas

Ingredients:
2 cups Corn Tortilla Powdered Mix
2 cups water

Preparation:
Heat an 8 inch or larger cast iron pan over a medium fire with no oil. Have a container about the same size with lid available.

Mix the tortilla powder mix with water until there is an even mix that resembles clay. Take a small pinch of the tortilla clay (about 4 tablespoons) and roll into a ball in between your hands. Then begin to flatten out by slapping it into shape between your open flat hands. Once you've reached the desired look place in pan and allow to toast up on one side then flip tortilla once and allow the same to the other side. Then remove tortilla from pan and place in container and seal. This allows the tortilla to steam itself to softness. Wrapping them in a small kitchen towel works as well. Repeat this process until all the tortilla mix is gone. The stack of tortillas will keep each other warm as long as you keep them wrapped in a towel or a sealed container or both. As soon as you've put away the last one they're ready to serve.

Recipe by: Brian Espanoza

Flat Bread Spinach Feta Pizza

Serves 6-8

Ingredients:
1 package active dry yeast (0.25 oz)
1 1/2 tsp. sugar
1 cup warm water (105 degrees to 115 degrees)
2 Tbsp. butter or margarine, softened
1 1/2 tsp salt
2 1/2 cups all-purpose flour
1/2 cup Gruyere cheese
1/2 cup feta cheese
1 oz. Fresh basil leaves
6 oz. Fresh baby spinach leaves
2 Tbsp. olive oil

Preparation:
In a warm mixing bowl, dissolve yeast in warm water and sugar. Stir in enough flour to form a stiff dough and add salt. Turn onto a floured surface; knead until smooth and elastic, about 4 minutes. Place in a greased bowl, turning once to grease top. Cover and let rise in a warm place until doubled, about 45 minutes. Punch dough down. Divide in half. Roll each half out to form a pizza shape.

Preheat oven to 400°. Brush some of the olive oil onto dough. Spread chunks of Gruyere cheese on top. Spread feta on top of Gruyere. In large bowl toss basil and spinach with remaining oil and chili flakes. Pile mixed leaves on top of dough and place in preheated oven for 15-20 minutes, or until the spinach is cooked down and the pizza is golden brown. Cut and serve.

Recipe by: Brian Espanoza

Leeks Au Gratin

Serves 6

Leeks carry a lot of moisture, although it isn't apparent at first glance. We must remember to consider this when assembling the dish. This dish is very simple, quick, and delicious.

Ingredients:
2 large leeks
1 cup Monterey Jack cheese
1 cup heavy whipping cream
salt & pepper

Preparation:
Preheat oven to 350°. On a cutting board, score leeks lengthwise from tip to tail, cutting down to the center of the leek but not deep enough to cut the leek in half. Rinse out any mud left inside the leaves of the leek. Once they are clean, cut them into 2" thick medallions and set them on end into a 9"x12" deep dish pan. Make sure that they are nice and snug in the pan so that they don't fall over.

Add a little salt by sprinkling it over the leeks. Add the cream by drizzling it over every leek, making sure each piece gets a portion of the cream. Sprinkle most of the cheese over the entire dish, but hold a handful aside for later. Sprinkle with freshly ground pepper. Cover the dish with aluminum foil, making sure the foil does not touch the surface of the leeks and cheese. Place dish in the pre-heated oven and bake for 40 minutes. Then remove the foil and sprinkle the remaining cheese over the top. Return dish to the oven and allow the top to crisp up and turn a golden color. We are now ready to serve.

Recipe by: Brian Espanoza

Mushroom Stroganoff

Serves 6

Ingredients:
2 Tbsp vegetable oil
1/4 cup olive oil
1 large onion, chopped
1 1/2 tsp dried tarragon
1 1/2 tsp dried dill
1 1/4 pounds mushrooms, sliced
2 cups vegetable broth
2 cups sour cream
1/4 cup chopped fresh parsley
1/2 lb. tofu, pressed and cut into 1" cubes (optional)
Salt & Pepper to taste
1 pound pasta

Preparation:
Cook pasta in boiling salted water according to package directions.

Heat vegetable oil in large skillet. Add tofu cubes and saute until brown on all sides. Remove tofu.

Warm olive oil in skillet. Add onions; saute for 7-10 minutes, until soft. Add tarragon, dill, and mushrooms. Saute until mushrooms are moist. Add enough vegetable broth to barely cover. Simmer on medium-low heat until flavors meld and liquid reduces. Remove from heat and blend in sour cream. Add tofu. Return to low heat, but do not let it boil. When sauce is heated and thick, stir in tofu and parsley, and salt and pepper to taste. Pour over pasta and Serve.

Recipe by: Marti Waite

Potatoes Au Gratin

Serves 8

Ingredients:
8 potatoes
1/4 cup butter
1/2 cup flour
1 1/2 cups milk
1 1/2 cups Swiss cheese, shredded
A pinch of fresh ground nutmeg
Salt & Pepper

Preparation:
Preheat oven to 350°. Peel potatoes and slice as thin as possible with a knife or a mandolin. Slice potatoes directly into a bowl of cool water and set aside. Shred cheese and set aside. Next, in a pot that will fit the potatoes begin to melt butter over medium high flame on stove. When it has completely melted add the flour and mix thoroughly until it forms a paste. Next add the milk and loosen up the paste. As soon as the paste is softened add 2/3 of the shredded Swiss cheese and remove from flame. If you have access to a micro-plane take a whole nutmeg and grate a pinch of nutmeg into the cheese mixture. Add salt and pepper.

Next strain the potatoes. Give the potatoes a quick rinse to remove excess starch and place place back into the bowl. Now take the cheese mixture and pour over potatoes and gently fold together so as not to smash the thin potato slices.

Next place the potatoes into an oiled 9"x12" casserole dish or deep gratin dish. Sprinkle the remaining cheese over the mixture and place the dish in the preheated oven and bake for 1 hour. Remove from oven when the surface is a golden brown.

Recipe by: Brian Espanoza

Ratatouille

Serves 6

Ingredients:
3 zucchinis, cut into 1" diagonal pieces
2 red bell peppers, cut into 1" squares
1 lg. eggplant, unpeeled and cut into 1" cubes
2 carrots, cut into 1" diagonal pieces
1 yellow onion, cut into 1" cubes
1/4 cup diced parsley
1/4 cup diced basil
1/2 cup tomato paste
1/4 cup honey
salt & pepper
4 Tbsp vegetable oil

Preparation:
Preheat oven to 350°. Cut all vegetables and toss together with the oil and lightly salt and pepper. Spread onto a sheet pan and place into oven for 20-25 minutes, until vegetables are caramelized and cooked through, but still holding their shape.

Once vegetables have caramelized, take them out of the oven and toss in the tomato paste, honey, and fresh diced herbs. Salt and pepper to taste. Serve in casserole.

Recipe by: Brian Espanoza

Risotto Milanessa

Serves 6

Ingredients:
3 cups Arborio rice
3 Tbsp olive oil
1 large yellow onion, diced fine
2 garlic cloves, thinly sliced
1 cup parsley, diced fine
9 cups vegetable stock
2 Tbsp saffron
2 1/2 cups grated Parmesan cheese
Salt & Pepper to taste

Preparation:
Heat oil in a medium sized saucepan over medium heat. Simmer the onion in the oil for about 10 minutes. When the onion is soft, add garlic and rice.

Saute the rice in the pan with the onion and garlic over medium heat for 5 to 7 minutes, or until lightly toasted. Stir constantly so the rice will not stick and burn. Stir in one ladle of vegetable stock, and keep stirring until it is mostly absorbed, ladling and stirring in more of the broth in the same manner, until the rice is almost al dente. Stir in the saffron, 1 cup parsley, salt and pepper, and 3/4 cup of Parmesan cheese. Turn off the heat, cover and let sit for 4 or 5 minutes then serve.

Recipe by: Brian Espanoza

Romesco Sauce

Ingredients:
4 roma (plum) tomatoes, halved
1 large red bell pepper, quartered
7 cloves garlic
1/3 cup and 1 tablespoon olive oil
salt to taste
2 large slices old sourdough bread (any kind of simple bread)
1/4 cup and 2 teaspoons toasted whole almonds
1/4 cup and 2 teaspoons red wine vinegar
1/4 teaspoon Spanish paprika
pinch crushed red pepper flakes, or to taste

Preparation:
Preheat oven to 425°.
Place the tomatoes, bell pepper, and garlic cloves into an oiled casserole (glass or ceramic is fine). Brush the vegetables with some of the olive oil, then sprinkle with salt. Bake in the preheated oven until the garlic has turned golden brown, 25 to 35 minutes. Remove from the oven, and allow to cool for 10 minutes. While the vegetables are cooling, fry the bread slices on well oiled pan until golden brown on both sides. Remove and allow to cool.

Scrape the vegetables and any juices from the pan into a food processor or blender. Break the bread into pieces, and add to the food processor along with the toasted almonds, vinegar, paprika, and red pepper flakes. Puree until finely ground, then drizzle in the remaining olive oil with the machine running. Season to taste with additional salt if necessary.

Recipe by: Brian Espanoza

Ron's Nutloaf

serves 4-6

Ingredients:
1 1/4 cups cooked brown rice
¼ cups uncooked rolled oats
5 cups mushrooms, chopped
1 small onion, chopped
2 cloves garlic, chopped
2 lg. eggs, beaten
3/4 cups cheese (any type)
1 1/4 cups roasted walnuts and cashews
5 Tbsp. thyme
2 1/2 Tbsp. fresh parsley
1 1/4 tsp. dried oregano
1 1/4 tsp. fennel seeds
1 tsp. red pepper flakes
3 Tbsp. olive oil or butter
2 tsp soy sauce
Salt & Pepper to taste

Preparation:
Preheat oven to 350°. Sauté onions, mushrooms and garlic with oil and herbs. Drain and set aside. Roast walnuts and cashews for 10 minutes. Pureé mushrooms and onions with roasted nuts in food processor. Add salt, pepper, and soy sauce to mixture to taste. Add more herbs if desired. Add eggs and cheese to mixture. Add cooked brown rice and oats. Put mixture into greased baking pan. Bake for 30 minutes covered and 15 minutes uncovered.

Best served with mashed potatoes and mushroom gravy.

Recipe by: Ron Malanga

Rinpoche's Momo Recipe

Serves 4-6

Momos are Tibetan dumplings filled with stuffing and steamed or boiled. There are thousands of variations on the stuffings; it's fun to experiment and find the flavors that you like the most. The finished dumpling is similar in shape to a Chinese pot sticker, but they are usually steamed or boiled rather than fried. Making momos is best done in the company of others and although making beautiful momos is an art form, ugly momos taste just as good!

Ingredients:

4-5 cups flour
1 1/2 cups water
1 16oz. packet frozen chopped spinach
2 bundles fresh mint, minced
2 6oz. packets feta cheese
6 portabella mushrooms
2-4 6oz. pieces fresh mozzarella
1/2 cup grated parmesan
Olive oil

Preparation:

First, prepare the dough.
Place 4 cups of flour in a large bowl. Slowly add water, mixing well, until all the water is absorbed. Add more flour, if needed, to make a smooth ball of dough. Knead the dough for a few minutes; then place in a clean, oiled bowl and cover. Let it sit for at least 15 minutes at room temperature.

Next, prepare the filling.
Rinse spinach in room temperature water and squeeze out all excess moisture with your hands. Allow to drain while you assemble the other ingredients.

Chop feta, mozzarella and mushrooms finely, or cut together in a food processor.

Combine drained spinach, mint, cheeses and mushrooms in a

large bowl. Using your hands, mix well. Stir in a generous amount of good olive oil. Cover and refrigerate filling until ready to use.

Roll out the dough into one long log. Cut in half lengthwise. Roll into thin logs, about one-inch wide. Chop dough into small pieces, about 1/2" long each, forming circles. Flatten circles, then roll with a rolling pin into thin circles. Cover with a towel to prevent the dough from drying out.

Then, putting the filling in the dough.
Hold one circle in your left hand. Spoon one tablespoon of filling onto the dough. Bring the edges of the dough together and pinch together into a half-moon shape. Alternatively, you can use a pulling and pinching motion to bring the dough over the filling and pinch together at the top. Place assembled momos on a non-stick surface and cover with a slightly damp towel to prevent them from drying out.

Cooking:

Pour two inches of water into the bottom of a steamer and bring to a boil. Add one layer of momos in each section of the steamer. Cover and steam for about 10 minutes. Serve hot with hot sauce and soy sauce.

Alternate Cooking:

Momo Soup: If you don't have a steamer, you can boil momos in a soup: saute some onions (not if on precepts diet) and tomatoes in olive oil. Add vegetable broth or water, soy sauce, and any vegetables that sound good. Bring to a boil. Add momos; simmer for about 20 minutes or until momos rise to the top.

Fried Momos: You can also pan fry your momos with some oil on medium heat until the dough is golden brown.

Recipe by: Lama Zopa Rinpoche
(Written down with explanations
by Venerable Annette, "Thea" Cynthia Crossley
and Marti Waite)

Sweet & Sour tofu

Serves 4-6

Ingredients:
1 lb. tofu, cubed
3-4 stalks green onion, chopped
1 small red bell pepper, chopped
1/4 cup tomatoes, diced
1/3 cup balsamic vinegar
1/3 cup brown sugar
1 tsp red pepper flakes
1 Tbsp sesame oil
1/4 cup onions, chopped
1 tbsp ginger, chopped
1/2 tsp salt
3/4 cup water or veg. stock
1/4 cup cornstarch dissolved in 3/4 cup water

Preparation:
Combine the tomatoes, vinegar, sugar, red pepper flakes, and salt in a bowl.

Boil a pan of water. Sprinkle in salt, reduce to a simmer and add cubed tofu. Simmer for 5 minutes, and drain.* Heat a large skillet, then add the oil. Add the onions; stir fry for 2 minutes; Add peppers and ginger and stir fry for 1-2 minutes. Add the tomato mixture, chopped scallions, and stock or water. Simmer for about 5 minutes, then add the tofu and cornstarch mixture. Cook until the sauce is thickened and the tofu is heated through, several minutes more. Salt to taste.
* For more texture, tofu can also be fried or roasted.

Recipe by: Brian Espanoza

Tofu Mole

Serves 6

Ingredients:
4 lbs. extra firm tofu
3 Tbsp chili powder (mild)
1/4 cup tamari (soy sauce)
6 Tbsp vegetable oil
1/4 cup finely chopped onion
2 Tbsp unsweetened cocoa powder
1-1/2 tsp ground cumin
4 Tbsp sesame seeds
1/4 cup peanuts
1/2 tsp dried minced garlic
1 cup tomato paste
1/4 cup agave nectar
1 Ancho chili
1 1/2 cups water

Preparation:
Preheat oven to 375°. Prepare the tofu for roasting by cutting tofu into 1" chunks. Place tofu in a large mixing bowl. Add tamari, chili powder, and 5 Tbsp oil. Sprinkle with salt and pepper, and toss it all together, mixing well. Spread across a large oiled sheet pan. Place pan into the preheated oven for about 30 minutes until tofu is crisp and brown.

Meanwhile, we can prepare our mole. There are many ways to prepare mole and there are quite a few different styles of moles. This is a traditional Aztec sauce that can be found throughout the southwest in a variety of interpretations. (Continued on next page)

Begin by heating a large sauce pan on the stove and add 1 tbsp. oil. Once the oil is hot, add the onions. Cook until translucent and add garlic, sesame seeds, peanuts and cumin. Next add 1 1/2 cups of water, the tomato paste and Ancho chili. Bring the mixture to a boil and then reduce heat to a light simmer. Allow this to simmer for about 20 minutes while tofu is roasting.

Remove the roasted tofu from the oven and with a metal spatula remove tofu from pan without losing too much of the caramelized tofu that was in contact with the pan. Pour into a casserole dish.

Strain out all the ingredients from the mole broth. Place our strained ingredients into a blender and slowly add enough of the broth till we have a thick creamy texture. Now add the agave syrup and season with salt and pepper to taste.

Pour the creamy mole sauce over the tofu casserole. Sprinkle 1 tsp of toasted sesame seeds over the mole and serve.

Recipe by: Brian Espanoza

Agua Fresca

Ingredients:
1/2 honeydew melon, peeled and seeded
4 tablespoons of agave syrup
16 cups of water

Preparation:
Blend water, melon and syrup until smooth in a blender. Chill and serve.

Recipe by: Brian Espanoza

LMB Chai

serves 8-10

Ingredients:
6 cups boiling water
4-5 black tea bags
2 tsp cardamom (freshly ground)
1 ½ cups whole milk
1 ½ cups soy milk
Sugar or agave nectar

Preparation:

Boil water. Add the tea bags and cardamom. Boil for one minute. Add milk. Add sugar or agave nectar to taste. Stir and simmer, covered, for 15-20 minutes.

Strain tea through a fine mesh strainer and serve.

Recipe by: Cynthia Crossley (Thea)

Banana Scones

Serves 8

Ingredients:
1 cup white rice flour
1/2 cup tapioca flour
1/2 tsp xanthan gum
2 tsp baking powder
1 tsp baking soda
4 tbsp margarine
3 bananas
3/4 cup walnuts
1/2 cup soy milk or almond milk

Preparation:
Preheat oven to 400°. Grease 1 baking sheet.
In a medium mixing bowl, whisk together the flours, xanthan gum, baking powder, and baking soda. Add the margarine and cut it into the mix using a fork or knife, until the mix has the texture of cornmeal. Add the bananas and walnuts. Then add milk until all ingredients clump together, forming a stiff dough.

Scoop out even portions of dough with a 2 oz. ice cream scoop and drop onto greased baking sheet. Then press each scoop with a fork to give each portion a nice form. Place in oven and bake for 25-30 minutes or until golden brown spots form on surface. Serve immediately.

Recipe by: Brian Espanoza

Cornbread

Yields 12 pieces

Ingredients:
1 cup cornmeal
1 cup flour
1/2 tsp. salt
1/2 Tbsp. baking powder
2 eggs
1/2 cup corn oil or vegetable oil
1/4 cup honey
1 cup milk

Preparation:
Preheat oven to 400 degrees. Oil square baking pan or 9" cake pan with cooking spray, butter, or oil. Stir dry ingredients and make a well in the bowl. In separate bowl, whisk wet ingredients. Quickly mix wet and dry, pour into pan and bake in the middle of oven until golden brown on top and pulling away from edges, about 20 minutes. Serve warm.

Recipe by: William Becking (Vimal)

Honey Whole Wheat Bread
Yields 1 Loaf

Ingredients:
3 cups warm water (105°)
1 1/2 Tbsp yeast
1 1/2 Tbsp sugar
3 cups all purpose flour
3 cups whole wheat flour
1/2 cup sunflower seeds
1 cup extra whole wheat flour (for kneading)
1/2 cup honey
1 cup scalded milk
2 tsp salt
1/2 egg

Preparation:
Preheat oven to 350°. In a warm metal mixing bowl combine 3 cups warm water with yeast and sugar and whisk vigorously. Allow to rest for 3-5 minutes for the yeast to activate. Meanwhile, heat milk over medium-low heat until it foams up. Remove from heat. Allow the milk to cool for a couple of minutes and then mix with honey. Once a rich lather has formed on top of the yeast add the scalded milk and honey and whisk together.

Next add the flours, sunflower seeds, and the salt and mix until you have a nice dough formed. Leave in bowl to rise for 40-45 minutes. Then remove from bowl and drop onto work surface, using extra flour to keep from sticking to the surface. Knead dough into a loaf and place on sheet pan lined with parchment paper. Beat egg vigorously and over the top of the dough. Then score the top of the loaf with a sharp knife. This will allow the bread to expand upward rather than out the sides. It also gives it a nice looking surface after it's baked. Bake for 40-45 minutes or until the surface is a dark golden brown and has a hollow sound to the tap. Allow to rest for at least 30 minutes before slicing in to it.

Recipe by: Brian Espanoza

Breads

Olive Country Bread

Yields 1 loaf

Ingredients:
3 cups warm water (105°)
1 1/2 Tbsp yeast
1 1/2 Tbsp sugar
3 cups all-purpose flour
3 cups whole wheat flour
2 cups Kalamata olives
1/2 cup olive oil
1/2 cup molasses
1 cup all purpose flour
1/2 Tbsp salt

Preparation:
Preheat oven to 350°. In a warm metal preparation bowl combine 3 cups warm water with yeast and sugar and whisk vigorously. Allow to rest for 3-5 minutes for the yeast to activate. Once a nice lather has formed on the surface combine with all the flour, olives, olive oil, molasses, and salt.

Allow to rise for 40-45 minutes. Cover your work surface with remaining 1 cup of flour. Turn out your dough and knead into a long football shaped loaf. Place the loaf on a baking pan lined with parchment paper. Use the remainder of the flour on the table to completely cover the loaf leaving it white and completely dusted. Score the loaf straight down the middle lengthwise and bake in preheated oven for 40-45 minutes. To check if the loaf is ready tap it with your finger. If it sounds hollow it's ready. Remove from oven and allow to rest for 30 minutes or so before slicing.

Recipe by: Brian Espanoza

Chocolate Brownies

Ingredients:
5 oz semisweet chocolate
1/2 cup + 1 Tbsp cocoa powder
2 Tbsp vegetable oil
1/2 cup unsalted butter
3 large eggs
1 1/4 cups sugar
2 tsp vanilla
1/2 tsp salt
1 cup unbleached white flour

Preparation:
Preheat oven to 350.
Melt the chocolate, butter, oil, and cocoa powder in a double broiler, then set aside to cool.

In an 8" baking pan fold four layers of tin foil (best with two double layered pieces) into pan.

Whisk together eggs, sugar, vanilla, and salt. Mix in chocolate mixture. Use a wooden spoon to mix in the flour till just combined. Pour into baking pan. Bake for 35-40 minutes or until toothpick inserted into middle comes out with tiny sticky crumbs. Cool on rack for 2 hours (works great in the fridge to cool it off).

Recipe by: Philip Collins

Chocolate Pudding

Serves: 6

Ingredients:
2 Tbsp. cornstarch
1/4 cup sugar
1/4 cup cocoa
1 2/3 cup whole milk
14 oz. semisweet chocolate, finely chopped
1 Tbsp. unsalted butter

Preparation:
Whisk together cornstarch, 1/4 cup sugar, 1/4 cup cocoa, and a pinch of salt in a heavy saucepan or double boiler, then gradually whisk in milk. Bring to a boil, whisking constantly, then boil, whisking, until thickened. Remove from heat and whisk in chopped chocolate and butter until melted. Dish into 6 ramekins or cups and chill until served, at least 1 hour.

Recipe by: Vimal

Pumpkin Brownies

Yield: 16 brownies

Ingredients:
Make Fudge Brownie Batter:
1/2 cup cocoa powder
1/4 cup butter
scant 1/2 cup canola oil
1 cup brown sugar
1/2 tsp vanilla
3 lg eggs
1/2 cup flour

Preparation:
Preheat Oven to 350 Degrees.
Melt butter and combine with cocoa powder and oil. Mix in brown sugar and vanilla, and beat well!

Add the eggs, mixing until well combined. Pour in the flour, mixing into a smooth batter. Butter a square pan and pour in the mixture.

Then Make Pumpkin Goodness:
1/2 cup organic pureed pumpkin
3 Tbsp sweetened condensed milk or evaporated milk
1 egg
1/4 tsp cinnamon

Beat the egg slightly. Add all the ingredients together in a pan. On medium heat stir the mix for 2-3 minutes until creamy.

Pour the pumpkin mix on top of the brownie mix. Swirl the pumpkin mix into just the top of the brownie mix. Bake for 25-35 minutes until the brownies start to «peel» away from the edges of the pan.

Recipe by: Philip Collins

Vegan, Wheat Free, and Precepts Safe

We are well aware of individual people having specific dietary needs. We try to cater to the many needs of our staff and guests here at Land of Medicine Buddha. Though there are many types of food allergies and preferences we have organized this cookbook to note recipes that are Vegan, Wheat Free and safe for the 8 Mahayana Precepts diet.

Please note that in almost every one of the recipes in this book, substitutions can be made to accommodate your specific needs. Those who are vegan can use non-dairy and non-animal-based ingredients in place of non-vegan ingredients. Such as Earth Balance (vegan butter substitue), soy milk in place of milk, and agave nectar instead of honey. Those who are wheat free can substitute wheat flower with rice flour, garbanzo bean flower or whichever suits your taste. Those people who are living in the vows of the 8 Mahayana Precepts can use celery in place of onion and ginger in place of garlic in most cases. There are also vegan egg substitutes that can be used for precept diets. So, feel free to experiment and alter these recipes to fit your dietary preferences. Enjoy!

Cooking with Bodhichitta Mindfulness

by Gelongma Losang Drimay

Lama Zopa Rinpoche emphasizes that we should not waste any opportunity for Dharma practice. We can turn even our ordinary everyday activities into Dharma—the causes for enlightenment—by combining them with certain positive thoughts. Bodhichitta is the mind of a bodhisattva having the intent to become a buddha for the sake of all sentient beings. Bodhichitta mindfulness consists of thoughts of benefiting others, specifically by leading them out of suffering and delusion and leading them to enlightenment. In that process, there are many things to be purified and other things to be actualized. Rinpoche has done some cooking demonstrations explaining how to think when we do each part of the preparation, but once you get the idea you can come up with some of your own slogans. Here are some examples of Rinpoche's bodhichitta mindfulness sayings.

Begin your cooking with a bodhichitta motivation: "By this action of cooking, I am leading all sentient beings to enlightenment. May I cherish all sentient beings immediately and free them from every suffering. May all their suffering come onto the 'I' and may they receive all the happiness."

Then combine each step with a related mindfulness, like this:

While peeling vegetables, think, "I am taking off sentient beings' delusions."

While shredding vegetables, think, "I am destroying self-cherishing thought."

While adding flour to a broth, think, "I am adding realizations."

While stirring a mixture (such as the filling for momos), think, "I am taming sentient beings' minds."

While rolling out dough (such as momo wrappers), think, "I am eliminating mistaken thoughts toward the guru."

While pinching the dough together (such as the momo wrapper around the filling), think, "I am gathering together the five paths and the ten bhumis (the levels of realization on the way to buddhahood)."

Let your good heart be your guide.

Buddhist Offering Prayers

As we are a Tibetan Buddhist Retreat center we thought it would be nice to include these food offering prayers in English and with Tibetan phonetics for those who are so inclined.

Sometimes it can be very difficult to eat mindfully, especially when the food is delicious. Starting a meal with a food offering prayer can be a good way to remind us to eat more mindfully. Even if we do loose our mindfulness after a couple of bites, it is still meaningful to think of the Guru, Buddha, Dharma, and Sangha before we eat.

Before you begin to eat, you could take a minute to look at your food and reflect on how many people worked so that you can have this meal. The farmers, people in the stores, people who prepared your food, etc.

OM AH HUM - *(Recite three times. This represents the enlightened body speech and mind of the Buddhas and our own potential.)*

TÖN PA LA ME SANG GYÄ RIN PO CHHE
To the supreme teacher, the precious Buddha,
KYAB PA LA ME DAM CHHÖ RIN PO CHHE
To the supreme refuge, the precious Dharma,
DREN PA LA ME GE DÜN RIN PO CHHE
To the supreme guides, the precious Sangha,
KYAB NÄ KÖN CHHOG SUM LA CHHÖ PA BÜL
To the Triple Gem, the objects of refuge, I make offering.

LA MA SANG GYÄ LA MA CHHÖ
The Guru is Buddha, the Guru is Dharma,
DE ZHIN LA MA GE DÜN TE
The Guru is Sangha also.
KÜN GYI JE PO LA MA TE
The Guru is the creator of all (happiness).
LA MA NAM LA CHHÖ PAR BÜL
To all gurus, I make this offering.

Mahayana Precepts Diet

In the Buddhist Mahayana tradition there is a specific practice where the practitioner takes specific vows for 24 hours at a time out of compassion for all beings. This practice is suitable for members of the monastic community as well as lay people.

"Upon taking the Eight Mahayana Precepts, one must avoid black foods, such as meat, eggs, garlic and onions, and eat food of the three white substances before noon, in one sitting, and not get up to take a second helping. One must then abandon eating food at the wrong time—from noon that day until sunrise the next." - from *Direct and Unmistaken Method*, By Kyabje Lama Zopa Rinpoche

Some monastics (monks and nuns) choose to keep the precept diet all the time. Some lay Buddhist practitioners also decide to keep this diet to support their spiritual practice. While others may decide observe the precepts only on holy days. Some Buddhists are vegetarian while others are not.

If you are interested in learning more about taking the Eight Mahayana Precepts visit (http://www.fpmt.org/prayers/8precepts.php). Please note that the first time one takes the precepts, it is taken from a master who holds the lineage. Thereafter, one can do the ceremony before a Buddha image by regarding it as the actual Buddha.

About Land of Medicine Buddha

Land of Medicine Buddha is a green certified, and pet friendly, non-profit retreat center located in Santa Cruz County offering Buddhist classes and retreats, space for personal retreats, as well as rental facilities for private groups to hold their own spiritual workshops, conferences, and trainings.

The goal of our Center, based on the principles taught by Shakyamuni Buddha and promoted worldwide by His Holiness Dalai Lama, is to nurture healing and the development of a good heart, which includes the cultivation of compassion and loving kindness. As such, the center aspires to teach principles for living that are universally applicable.

Besides offering classes, retreats and rituals relating to the study and integration of Buddhist practices in our daily life...

We have 108 acres of redwood forest and a peaceful meadow for hiking and meditation; genuine customer service performed by a team dedicated to your happiness; simple and comfortable rooms with private bathrooms; vegetarian cuisine using organic products whenever possible, prepared freshly and cooked with love by a team of professional chefs.

We have a meditation hall which provides a harmonious setting for transformational classes and retreats, in the presence of inspirational life size statues and paintings of Buddhas and deities, and a Sand Mandala complete with a multitude of water bowl offerings.

Land of Medicine Buddha was established in 1983 by two

Tibetan Buddhist masters, Lama Thubten Yeshe and Lama Zopa Rinpoche. It was their vision for Land of Medicine Buddha to be a place of ultimate healing. We are affiliated with FPMT, Foundation for the Preservation of the Mahayana Tradition, an international organization of 147 Centers and social projects worldwide.

Our center is proud to support the preservation of the Tibetan cultrure. We feel blessed to be helping keep alive amazing Tibetan art forms, as is seen in our Wish Fulfilling Temple, Gompa, Statues, Stupas and Prayer Wheels.

We continue to reach out to the the local community in a variety of ways including our annual festivals, supporting Tara Redwood School (a great local school for young children teaching the values of love and compassion), and Tara Home (a boarding home offering end of life care offered by a team of trained volunteers).

Sustainability and non-harming is important to us and we are certified "green" with the Monterey Bay Green Business Program. Our center is engaged in many inspiring projects including upgrading of facilities to be more environmentally conscious, improving accessibility to our buildings, creating our own organic vegetable garden, and building a magnificent stupa for world peace.

Please visit our website at:
www.landofmedicinebuddha.org

Please visit our retreat center at:
Land of Medicine Buddha
5800 Prescott Road
Soquel CA 95073
USA

CPSIA information can be obtained at www.ICGtesting.com
Printed in the USA
LVOW080746240612

287392LV00006B/24/P